Some Problems with Autobiography

Some Problems with Autobiography

POEMS

Brian Brodeur

WINNER OF THE NEW CRITERION POETRY PRIZE

Criterion Books
NEW YORK

First American edition published in 2023 by Criterion Books, an imprint of Encounter Books, an activity of Encounter for Culture and Education, Inc., a nonprofit, tax-exempt corporation.

www.newcriterion.com/poetryprize
www.encounterbooks.com

Manufactured in the United States and printed on acid-free paper. The paper used in this publication meets the minimum requirements of ANSI/ NISO Z39.48–1992 (R 1997) (*Permanence of Paper*).

LIBRARY OF CONGRESS CATALOGING-IN-PUBLICATION DATA

Names: Brodeur, Brian, 1978– author.
Title: Some Problems with Autobiography: Poems / Brian Brodeur.
Description: First American edition. | New York : Criterion Books, 2023. |
Identifiers: LCCN 2022041022 | ISBN 9781641773324 (hardcover) |
     ISBN 9781641773331 (ebook)
Subjects: LCGFT: Poetry.
LCC PS3602.R6347 S66 2023 | DDC 811/.6–dc23/eng/20220831
LC record available at https://lccn.loc.gov/2022041022

Contents

III

Acknowledgments

The author wishes to thank the editors of the following publications in which these poems, often in different versions, first appeared:

32 Poems: "Parents of Middle-Aged Children"
Able Muse: "On Mistaking a Stranger for a Dead Friend"
Blackbird: "Woman Waking Early in Late Fall"
The Cincinnati Review: "The Anthropocene Wing," "Exit Interview," and "Shared Wall"
Divining Dante (Recent Work Press, Australia): "On Being Mistaken for a Muslim," "The Pile," and "Tornado Season"
The Gettysburg Review: "Pessoa in the Rust Belt"
The Hopkins Review: "The Carpenter's Tale" and "Self-Portrait, 2085"
Image: "On Emptying a Deceased Relative's Home"
Literary Matters: "Barcode Ode," "Corn Poppets," "Space Junk," and "What We Told the Children"
The New Criterion: "On Not Baptizing My Daughter"
Smartish Pace: "Algorithm"
The Southern Review: "Some Problems with Autobiography"

"On Mistaking a Stranger for a Dead Friend" won the 2022 *Able Muse* Write Prize for poetry. "Barcode Ode," "Corn Poppets," and "Space Junk" won the 2020 Meringoff Award in Poetry from the Association of Literary Scholars, Critics, and Writers. "Algorithm" won third prize in the Nineteenth Annual Erskine J. Poetry Prize. "Mrs. Baumeister" was published in the chapbook *Local Fauna* (Kent State University Press, 2015).

Grateful acknowledgment is made to the following writers, editors, teachers, colleagues, and friends who provided invaluable feedback and encouragement: Jessica Anthony, Eric Bliman, Felix Burgos, Michelle Y. Burke, Dana Gioia, Heather Hamilton, Brian Patrick Heston, Ernest Hilbert, Keith Leonard, David Mason, Michael C. Peterson, Travis Rountree, Paul X. Rutz, Steve Scafidi, J. D. Scrimgeour, Christian Teresi, and Peter Vertacnik. A debt of gratitude is also owed to Indiana University East for providing invaluable leave time.

The author also wishes to thank the judges of the New Criterion Poetry Prize—Roger Kimball, Adam Kirsch, and Carmine Starnino—as well as the editors and publishers of Criterion Books, particularly Robert Erickson.

Finally, the author thanks his family, without whose love and support these poems would never have been written: Kiley Cogis Brodeur, Anna Brodeur, Regina Brodeur, Mark Brodeur, Erin Deslauriers, and Courtney Murphy.

For Kiley and Anna—my heart

I've lived in a state of mental slumber, leading the life of someone else. I've felt, very often, a vicarious happiness.

—Fernando Pessoa, *The Book of Disquiet*

Some Problems with Autobiography

Shared Wall

Lacrimae rerum

Jarred from our half-sleeping,
we hear its muffled chorus
past words, past caring for us,

and think the sheetrock's weeping.
Shrill sighs, like a rusty piston.
We press an ear to listen—

the burst of a yowled report
(our synapses misfiring
or the whining of old wiring)

dies down. How else to interpret
this noise that next door sings
except as the *yes* of things?

I

Algorithm

Then it could be the case that the vast majority of minds like ours do not belong to the original race but rather to people simulated by the advanced descendants of an original race.
—Nick Bostrom, "Are You Living in a Computer Simulation?"

I smirk until my smirking wilts to doubt—
how could I know I'm not? Knowing would be
part of the code the engineers worked out
as bits and bytes in high fidelity.
The implications sting: No you, no me.
No spouse or kids. No plot-point we'd accept
as plausible—nothing to think or see
we hadn't been preprogrammed for except
this: if our species is an avatar
doomed not to live but only interface,
it's not impossible this super-race
might grope through its own simulated night.
Unsure of what I glimpse in such faint light,
I squint: is that a satellite or star?

Triggered

Exodus Refugee Immigration Center
Indianapolis, Indiana, 2016

She hates living through history, she said.
She's seen an air-to-ground attack destroy
her neighborhood while her kids brushed for bed.

She knows what shrapnel does to the human head—
she helped bury her best friend's oldest boy
outside the breached exclusion zone they fled.

She's closed her own son's wounds with needle and thread
as he writhed in her arms gripping a legless toy,
thanking God next door got hit instead.

The night those barrel bombs left dozens dead,
she ran, riddled with flecks of steel alloy,
to flee the sarin gas before it spread.

Glass lodged in her bare feet as rooftiles shed
from buildings down the street. A bright convoy
of sirens passed. That's history, she said.

And I, the workshop volunteer who led
my session on "The Politics of Joy
in Poetry," if I'd never felt the dread

of drones equipped with thermal infrared
my own country continued to deploy
against a people made to beg for bread—

then who was I to say what should be said?

Barcode Ode

for J. L.

Checksum and glyph. Razor-slit gaps between
start-markers. Quiet zone. Each explains
everything it knows in silent lines
packed tight as eyelashes, the teeth of a comb,
a ventilator's bellow-squeeze become
stamp-sized. A city in fog, the skyline wan

from across the bay. If Blake saw flecks of sand
as worlds, what trapped infinities of ones
and zeroes might populate these X-dimensions
summoned by a cardinal chirp of light?
Never mind the snapped-on patient ID bracelet,
the IV needle's pinch as it descends.

Never mind how many hands have touched, dear friend,
your pulse, how the isolation gown-strings slip
open as you grope in and out of sleep.
Aware or not of what the RN says,
you wouldn't want even these sentences
catching you so prone. Forgive what words offend.

All message and no art, a means of meaning,
tight-lipped and bristly as a sutured mouth,
it can't deceive. Nor can it tell the truth
by containing multitudes, mute catalogs
dense as baleen, thin as a centipede's legs,
charred grove of matchsticks after rain still steaming.

The Carpenter's Tale

*There's going to be an accounting. And it'll be the weird stats
that come out of somewhere. And this is one of the stranger ones.*
—Kerry Breen, *This American Life*, August 3, 2021

Most of us laughed at being called "essential"
in those first weeks of New York's quarantine.
We'd grease a hinge or patch a rotten sill,

replacing sunk beams under a snack machine,
painting classrooms. Though it felt like cheating,
I'd never seen the schools look so pristine.

Then, in April, at our team meeting,
our boss clears his throat and his voice softens.
Putting down the cruller he's been eating,

he says, "Next week, we start building coffins."
One of us laughs. Another spills his coffee.
I tell my boss, "Get out of here. Build coffins."

He looks up from his clipboard and glares at me,
then gives us all the plans his boss gave him:
"We'll be building coffins for the city."

On Monday, I show up at this school gym
outfitted as a shop. On cinderblocks,
beside the bleachers with the lights turned dim,

our prototype: a six-foot plywood box
standing on its end where the feet would be.
Above the prototype and scoreboard clocks,

a championship banner's VICTORY
has begun to sag where flags of UN nations
clung to the ceiling. Under Germany,

we set up cutting and assembly stations,
a place where we could urethane the boards.
Electricians rig fans for ventilation

and ten of us plug in extension cords.
We stack up drafts of plywood on the floor—
a draft is fifty sheets. Our only words

concern the lack of Mets and Yankees scores,
how hot the gym gets, who brought Gatorade.
We run through two-by-fours and they bring more—

wash, rinse, repeat. I mean, we're getting paid,
but after so long it occurs to me:
my god, they really need this many made?

No one gives us an end. We build 150,
stacking them from one side of the gym
to the other, five coffins high—no one can see

above the shrink-wrapped freight pallets of them.
I drive the forklift out and take backstreets
to a tractor trailer near the stadium.

People honk at me. This goes on three weeks.
I find it—I don't know—bizarre, I guess,
not one person ever stops to ask me

what I'm doing, everyone obsessed
with toilet paper. Then, passing on foot,
a guy who speaks Spanish stops to zip his vest

and says, "*Morte*," finger-slicing his throat.
"*Sí*," I say, and he just shakes his head
and walks away. I slam the trailer shut.

Our team built 450 in the end,
and there were other teams in other districts
across the whole Department of Ed.

No one I tell has ever heard of this.
Why would they? Not exactly good PR—
Guess what we used schools for. You'll never guess . . .

But now that things are waning, more and more
I feel alright, like I can let it out.
It wasn't war—if it had been a war

we'd know what happened, what it was about,
how much we'd lost, what people did out there.
I'm sure someone will make a final count,

and we'll deal with each last expenditure,
but that's years off, and this is not a war.

On the Prospect of a Nuclear Exchange

Beach lots clear. Brake lights flare halogen reds
for miles. A hybrid's bumper sticker reads,
THE FUTURE'S NOTHING LIKE IT USED TO BE.
Untroubled by the cold seethe of the sea,
the sun, like a diving bell, starts to descend.
Gulls squabble as if arguing the end.
Kids burst outdoors before the dark redacts
dog parks and mudflats, the spires of smokestacks
spewing benzine smog and mercury.
The world is ever-ending. A dim geometry
of stars track-marking the sky above a pier
where meteors streak by and disappear.
A preacher in a bunker shuts his book
on Zacharia, Enoch, and Baruch.
In fields of orchard grass, gusts eddy.
A girl texts her best friend *I hate my body*
and pulls a weighted blanket over her.
Bug zappers spark. Her dad yells, "Are you here?"
The future's nothing, like it used to be.

Open Burning

As evening clouds bruise indigo,
our daughter asks us why
the leaves don't stay. We say they go
to make room for more sky.

She shrugs, then turns and stomps to dust
heaped leaves she gallops through.
Tossing armfuls up at us,
she screams, "I'll bury you."

Pessoa in the Rust Belt

A hunter of lions feels no adventure after the third lion. . . . If
I had impossible landscapes, what would I have left to dream?
—Fernando Pessoa, *The Book of Disquiet*

He gapes at a windfarm, its sprawling array
of steel stalks sprouting blades over the prairie—
    where *is* he? He asks but won't believe
this place isn't sacred, a shrine where mourners pray,

an aeronaut memorial rich townsfolk
commissioned, or the site where a prophet spoke
    of whirlwind scythes of fire portending
another apocalypse. Is it a joke?

A sign screams SAY NO TO GIANT TURBINES HERE
under these dozen churners of troposphere
    thrumming through their impossible dream
of cloud-shredding until ground and sky cohere.

He's not himself. Fresh contrails, slicing beneath
a day moon, mimic furrows in airy earth.
    Then thunderheads erase any trace
and muffle air-seeder chaff, the storm's wet breath

beginning to spit on so much borer blight
as on live embers, hissing, the pilot light
    of a bluebird perched in stripped branches.
These bare ash trees—they seem to *want* to ignite.

Is it always so fantastical? he asks.
The double rubber-mounted teeth of wheel rakes
        gnawing grass they turn into windrows,
meat raffles where church elders squeal, "Heaven sakes,"

their voices drifting here like an echoed hum
of *ecce homo* in fleece-clumped brambles some
        teenagers doused with stale motor oil
and burned instead of the "faggot" who ran home.

He says most days he feels like that limping boy.
Others, the boy's pursuers—both hedgerow bough
        and flame, the snarled wool flagging in wind
and the sheepdog chasing ewes that won't obey.

Fantastical? *Fantastique* comes closer still
to this froth of cottonwood seed, its pistils
        pale as seafoam, farms wide as small seas,
grain elevators like floating hospitals—

all of it performs on this phantasmal stage
as for the blacklisted of a former age:
        wrapped bales like marshmallows, this greenish
glaze of phosphorous that runoff creeks hemorrhage

as watersheds swell, tributaries forking
until they tangle taut as cat's-cradle string,
        the slack and strain of those frayed figures
passing between horizons, unraveling.

On Mistaking a Stranger for a Dead Friend

Bass River, South Yarmouth, Massachusetts

Where dozens of egrets feast
on their own reflection,
late streaks of sun
strike a surfcaster's face.
As he ties a jig lure,
I squint into the glare.

We'd fish this marsh as kids
for perch we called *kiver*,
a gang of us upriver
stomping swamp orchids
along a tidal island
of storm-washed sand.

In mud boots, I'd hike ahead
to scout a decent spot
on the crook of a silty spit.
Stumbling from a trailhead,
my friend, always last,
would swear he hadn't been lost.

I woke once to his voice,
his boy's voice calling still.
I leaned against the sill,
the window glazed with ice
dripping condensation,
and shut my eyes to listen.

Now, two egrets close
the kinked parentheses
of their necks, a damp breeze
sticking to my clothes.
Low tide's sulfur reek
fouls the estuary.

My friend's father, I learned,
found him in his apartment.
The father, who'd only meant
to stop by on an errand,
folded the typed note
and tried to untie the knot.

Shouldn't *egret* share a root
with *regret*? *Seem* with *seam*?
Swells at tideline gleam,
frothing algae-rot.
Though it urges hush, the surf
will not keep quiet itself.

One stalking egret weaves
through planks of an old pier.
Then, a juvenile pair
wades into grinding waves
that a last piling greets.
The beach crowds with regrets.

Parents of Middle-Aged Children

They can't be who they were when their kids were small,
and their kids can't forgive them for it now:
the hunch of their shoulders, a stiff hug's sour smell,
bones thin as kindling under a gauze of snow.

Should they be sorry for not having died?
For dropping devices they don't understand
when their kids with grown kids call confounded
by a son's loan, a daughter's wedding band?

The script is fixed. They won't explain themselves.
Like teens home late with hair shedding dried leaves,
they doubt the self could ever be explained.

See? They're still gnashing stones to make a spark,
trying for a little light against the dark
in woods they knew by heart until they changed.

To an Absence

The kid in latex gloves at Radford's Beef
brown-bags my five-pound brisket, saying, "Dude,
have a blessed day." I do the math—you'd be
a teenager, his age. Across the counter,
the brisket drips (the kid grinning, "My bad"),
but all I feel for you is gratitude
for the life your death allowed—my wife and daughter
I'd like one day to see I might deserve.
And *would* deserve, I think, if I could live
without the guilt I tongue like a decayed
incisor I've refused to have removed—
afraid what joy I've known might disappear
without a counter-pain to root it here.
The kid says, "Wait," and stamps my brisket PAID.

Space Junk

As if to remind us *orbit* rhymes with *obit*,
they chime colliding in low-Earth thermosphere
(chime, that is, if anyone here could hear),
this swarm of Kevlar and gold-foiled silicate.

Climbing the dark to predetermined heights,
they're abandoned, orphaned, multiplying, like us,
once they find each other, but by smashing to a fine dust,
a cloud of cold, unblinking satellites.

Unlike us, though, they stay sharp, stay afloat,
circling the same trajectory yet lost in a cyclical ring—
not a zero but a bellowed *O* murmuring,
a mouth droning hosannas loud and flat.

They were never born so can't be born again. Still,
they whorl cherubic in a rapture of scrap iron and
spare parts, awaiting whatever inscrutable command
issues from mission control in the smug high style

of *alpha* this, *omega* that. Miltonic bees poured forth
to cluster in halo vortices around our little blue hive,
they dive as if stirred by a single viscous heave,
sediment pulp and pap of celestial broth.

If pointed out one night in place of astral planes
to kids squinting through a compound scope ("Me!" "Me!"),
let their dad tweak the dials ("Now do you see?")
and herd them in a scrum around the lens.

Let the kids forsake the stars for this swirling spray
slicing the sky with swift sift and false fire,
no longer wanting what they were looking for
as one kid glimpses, bowing as if to pray,

two GEOS locking antennae beside Orion,
circulating, bright as dimes, flaring to life
with each clamor and snick in solar wind as if
plotting to populate some other modest stone.

Distance Learning

Her morning work involves a thunderstorm—
a negative and positive charge make
the lightning blink and thunder shake the room.
She spells *cloud* "clod." He says they need a break.
Why does he look outside each time he speaks?
He's tired. She still has rocket math to do.
Rain on the window threads thick silken streaks—
she asks him why. Because he told her to.
When gusts buffet their backyard's rotting fence,
she says she wishes Mondays were Mom's days.
Lightning burns hotter than the sun, they read,
but how do light and sound have their own speed?
Nothing makes sense. She slaps the page. He says
it's science—why should it make any sense?

II

The Anthropocene Wing

Somewhere ages and ages hence . . .

What little we've reclaimed of what they were
has become its name, a confection for the ear.
Bush cricket. Pupfish. Amur tiger. Man.
We think these two divergent trendlines mean
the rise of this one species brought the fall
of all else: elm trees, breeds of waterfowl.
At first, we blamed a meteor, but now
strong evidence suggests the white rhino
and damselfly—that mankind *wanted* this.
They drank the black blood of their god until
they drowned. We find them in the substrate still.
Look how the cranium of this one has
dry wells for eyes that seem to burrow down
and down, yet they don't see. Shall we move on?

The Pile

It seemed to happen then for all at once—
not *to* but *for*, a prognosis, a gift
none could refuse though many would renounce
as coruscating dust continued to drift

    and lodge particulates in eye and lung.
    Some watchers couldn't help trembling,

so they turned to glance around instead
at granite faces gaping at the scene.
Some stared at the ground where their shadows shed.
A newspaper. A door. A flashing screen.

    It happened as a chronic disenthralling—
    it happens still for those who can't look long

at images of charred concrete or beam,
for those who, even as it happened, knew
that day would shape whomever they'd become
when the pile was cleared. Gone are those people now

    who searched steel spandrels for the ones who'd flung
    their bodies from so high it looked like flying.

Some stalked hospitals. Some set down flowers—
carnations wrapped in crinkled cellophane—
where others had taped HAVE YOU SEEN ME fliers.
Some tried to reach the missing on the phone.

Some held the hands of strangers stopped along
the Armory fence the wind kept rattling.

This is who they were, an *us*, the ones who stayed
for a month, a week, a couple of days at least,
before the searing polymer reek gave way
to low-tide odors wafting from the east.

    Wading through the city's clamor and clang
      as through beached cargo or a stone dome falling,

some forgot the fires blazing there for weeks
below the streets, a smoldering cascade
that burned sunk joists and pilings down like wicks.
Some squinted at the blue that absence made,

    and felt unequal to the rubble's longing
    to be ash, the river's seaward lunge.

The Embrace

On winter break from college, she endured
a choppy prop-plane ride beside a man
whose breath suffused the air with the aroma
of offal rotting in the sun, a stench
that seemed to seep from deep within his bowels
like methane leaking from the arctic seabed.
More than once, she turned to wheeze into her fist—
what do you say to a stranger on a plane?
I'm sorry, sir, but could you please stop *breathing*?
Halfway between Columbus and Chicago,
a propeller stuttered and the plane bucked—
a boy laughed, an attendant shouted "Stop"
as luggage tumbled from the overheads.
The man touched her arm, "Please, pray with me?"
"Oh," she said, without meeting his eyes,
then met his eyes: his brow unfurrowing
as he droned above the hum of turboprops
his fetid invocations to the Lord.

When the plane regained control, she realized
she'd linked arms with the man, embracing him,
her left hand and his right hand interlaced.
More claws than hands—huge mutant crabs unshelled—
they made her own look insignificant
as he retracted them, apologizing,
then found his place in *Getting Well God's Way*
which he rested on his lap before he asked
if she'd accepted Jesus as her savior.
She stared at the seatback in front of her,

the wax-lined paper of the airsick bag.
He'd had the window seat—why'd he look *up*
to pray? Was thirty thousand feet not far
enough from Earth? She toggled through her phone.
He said he understood, his smile distorting
to a kind of inward wince, his yellow grin
like nacre on a string of antique pearls
he'd judged her undeserving to admire.
He licked his thumb, returning to his book.

They didn't speak again until they landed
when he handed her her satchel: "Merry Christmas!"
"You too," she offered, "Happy Holidays."
Rehearsing what she *should've* said, she fumed
and followed him as far as baggage claim
where he wheeled his carry-on into the men's.

On Not Baptizing My Daughter

I'd keep her faultless as the winter crow
pecking another crow smeared on the street,
not scaring as each passing car in snow
swerves to avoid it, and she asks me straight
if birds have souls. I laugh. Her face goes tense.
"Maybe," I say, and notice the soft sweep
of drifts has erased a neighbor's wire fence.
Crow-crowded pine boughs where the crows must sleep.
Hard to ignore their cackles or the brittle sound
of claws scraping the bleachers of the tree.
Their nattering in the hoarse-throat tongue of crows—
I could call it a cry, a scold, this caw that echoes
beyond their diet of what can be found,
but they're crows. They don't *behold* a scene. They see.

What We Told the Children

But are some acts so egregious as to be immune from the profit-motivated incentives to perpetuate them?
—"Money to Burn: Economic Incentives and the Incidence of Arson"

Just five words spoken through a tensed jaw
for Orpha Holzapfel, who still lives here,
who called each horse and held each muzzle near
to feed them mints before she lit the straw,
for the duty officer (her son-in-law)
who reached the stable first so he could clear
the scene and bribe the fire chief who, we'd hear,
would overlook the charred oil cans he saw
and click the ACT OF NATURE box without
approval or reproof but as one of us
who'd pass the paddock stacked with black barn-poles
on our way to pay respects with casseroles,
who'd chorus "Like a River, Glorious"
and tell our kids *the horses all got out.*

The Doll

Department of Social Services
Fitchburg, Massachusetts, 1988

When Mom transferred to Sexual Abuse,
she'd bring me to her office after school.
She'd fired the babysitter. I was nine.
I found a doll one day and started to play—
I knew it was a fake Cabbage Patch Kid,
but I was bored. Mom finished with her call.

She said the doll was "anatomical"—
a special toy with special parts she'd use
at interviews she had to have with kids.
She'd take them from their house or from their school.
Sometimes she had to watch them draw or play.
Sometimes she didn't leave work until nine.

She'd give the girls the girl doll named Jeanine.
The boys got Kid. (That's just what they were called.)
But they were only toys—I could still play.
Mom showed me how she'd teach the kids to use
the dolls—to point out, like a test in school,
the place where they'd been hurt. Unzipping Kid,

Mom sat him on her lap like a real kid.
He slumped. Mom asked if he was eight or nine—
did he like math or reading at his school?
She slid his jeans off. Anatomical.
His penis flopped. It looked like a cloth mouse.
His scrunched cloth testicles were on display.

I laughed. Mom said it wasn't time to play.
She made me promise someday if a kid
told me that he (or she) had been abused,
I'd go to her. Where did she keep Jeanine?
I checked drawers while Mom took another call.
I heard her say the name of my old school.

She circled on her notepad SOUTH STREET SCHOOL
and smiled at me, mouthing the words *go play*.
I hitched Kid's jeans up in the cubicle.
She slammed the phone and said another kid
whose stepfather . . . who wasn't even nine.
Then, she went quiet: those people who abused—

who *touched* their kids—deserved to be abused
themselves, in prison, poisoned with strychnine.
I asked why it was bad to touch a kid.

Tornado Season

Test sirens whine. A milky sky curdles to mud.
  Then thunder, grumbling in, souses glacial plains
    rumpled as bedsheets April rain unmade.
      Fields averse at first to furrow lines

surrender the rubble of last year's stubble stalks,
  and June steams in too soon with tumescent fumes
    of blossoms, grit from split-row planters, stacks
      of silage drying on dairy farms.

When *watch* updates to *warning*, panes click with gravel.
  The horizon primes and pulses coralline.
    Wind heaves its bloated gusts as blasts ravel
      debris, hardwoods buckle, signposts lean

to the ground, a golf cart dangles from naked eaves.
  The tempest seems intended, a screaming choir
    streaming in purple surges stripping leaves
      and clothes, particle board, a lawn chair.

Sure, meteorologists miss. But this, why this
  detritus drifting like fish-tank sediment
    smacking buildings, cars, a satellite dish
      swiveling through greenish firmament—

What have we done? the self-allegations begin.
  What misstep or slip, trespass or small offense
    brought on this fleet of airborne garbage bins,
      these poles impaling from a flung fence,

boats lodged in trees, whole corridors of corn taken,
  the all-clear stalled, the yowls, the mewls, the blackout,
    the news next day hard to accept and then
      common as the tongue in one's own mouth.

Mrs. Baumeister

The police came to me and said, "We are investigating your husband in relation to homosexual homicide.". . . I remember saying to them, "Can you tell me what homosexual homicide is?"
—Julie Baumeister, *People*, December 12, 1993

Thank you for seeing me on such short notice.
I've never had to hire a lawyer before,
and I don't think I really need one now—
Herb couldn't be the one who killed those boys.
The day our son brought home a human skull
he'd found behind our property, Herb said
it was the medical-school skeleton
his father, Dr. Baumeister, had owned.
Herb didn't know how else to dispose of it.

He's always been a conscientious man.
The Friesian foals we kept—when they broke free
or died, naturally, Herb was distraught.
He made a point to bury them himself—
he even bought a backhoe off a neighbor.
"There's one right tool for every job," he'd say.

I blame the Sav-a-Lot we owned in Muncie—
some weeks we wouldn't see him for three days.
He'd come home with dark bruises up his arms
from stocking shelves, unloading trailer pallets.
He'd gripe about the college kids he'd hired:
"Don't you get sick," he'd spit, "of all these faggots?"
"What faggots?" I'd ask. He'd stare at me.

This was around the time *The Star* reported
the Strangler of I-70, the one
police thought picked up hitchhikers—young men
he'd had *relations* with before they died.
I told Herb not to leave the house at night.
I'd hear him in the kitchen with his keys
rattling in his fist. He'd set them down
and pick them up again, rattling.

One morning, still dark, I woke to the odor
of woodsmoke. I found Herb's daybed empty—
a campfire blinking through our terrace trees.
In the backfield, he stood there in his boots,
just poking at the embers of a blaze
with a charred snow shovel. He was so sweaty.
I wanted to ask what he thought he was doing
outside without his coat, but I felt scared,
like I was interrupting, so I left.

I'm not *stupid*. But I have kids to raise,
my teaching job at New Joy Lutheran—
what could I say to make them understand?

Is that your wife and daughter on the desk?
Beautiful family. What would you do
if one of them—if you suspected something?
You'd fight to keep your family from harm.

If the wicked are rewarded, like Herb says,
all good people can do is find a place
to hide away and keep the world locked out.

He couldn't be the one—I don't believe
the things they say he did so many times.
How can you know a man twenty-three years
and not know him at all? Don't answer that.
I've taken too much of your day already.

Voicemail

He calls to tell her this will be the last
she'll hear from him—he thought she'd like to know.
Who has the time to think about the past?

He's married now. Two kids. Not like she asked.
Does she recall their trip to Mexico?
He knows he said his last call was the last,

but how could she forget that heat, how fast
those nights went talking on the patio?
He doesn't have the time now for the past,

to go back to that beach, sky overcast,
and race the rain to their cramped bungalow.
He called to tell her this time is the last—

he shouts the words again above the blast
of traffic blaring on the Triborough.
It's late. Too late to think about the past.

It's like that first beamed satellite broadcast
in space. Still echoing. He has to go.
He's telling her, though this call is the last,
he thinks they'll always make time for the past.

Days of 2018

That was the year my wife and I would *try*.
Rushing home from work at lunch, we'd strip
and hurry into bed. Then, spent, we'd rise
to share a bite before we had to leave.

After a while the mattress seemed to hiss
as our bodies throbbed together: *conceive, conceive*—
the soundtrack of some ancient rite of spring.

Once a month, she'd pee in a plastic cup
and dip the test stick into it and wait
with or without me for the faint pink stripe.
At first, she'd text me *Nothing*. Then she stopped.

We had a purpose, though, as if each kiss,
each fumbled nuzzle ("Hurry, babe, I'm late"),
were rendered honest as a hornet's sting.

***

My classes thinned. There'd been, the year before,
a week when campus closed and went online.
A man in hunting camo opened fire
but only hit the YOU BELONG HERE sign.

They couldn't find the guy to prosecute—
he'd sped his dirt bike through a thunderstorm.
The woods where he'd been hiding were clear-cut
and TeacherLocks installed in every room.

We'd crouch through active-shooter drills, lights out,
my students glowing in the smartphone glare.
We'd hug our knees. The floor gleamed like fake fruit.

Someone would muffle awkward laughs until
the undergrad who chewed her orange hair
would whisper *please*. He might be out there still.

***

The day the active shooter shot the sign,
I'd been there, in my office, oscillating
between the need to grade and urge to nap.

Scrunched under my desk clutching my phone,
I toggled from the campus-safety app
to my wife's texts insisting I'd be fine.

I had to pee. Bad. It was only fair—
to live a privileged life and die alone
among granola crumbs, a puddle of piss
commingling with the bloody gunk I'd pass.

I wouldn't call what I muttered a prayer,
but I slumped sweating on the carpet waiting
for the *pop* of rifle fire, repeating, "Let
it come, just when it does—not *this*, not yet."

***

Conceive, conceive—migrating sandhill cranes
would pipe it on their flyway over us.

I'd hear their diatonic bugle runs
and bolt outside to watch them clear the house.

As we sat down to salmon cakes one night,
I asked my wife: "Hey, isn't it too late?"

"For what?"
                    "The cranes—don't they migrate in fall?"

She woke her phone and pushed away her plate:
"It says they mate for life—the Cornell site."

I heard them call next day. A single crane
had drifted from the rest and seemed to stall
in shreds of fog. Descending through light rain,
it dropped too close to us—caught in headwinds—
I swear I heard the wet wheeze of its wings.

* * *

Weeks on, they found the guy near Hagerstown
living in the woods behind a church.

A hiker with his daughter saw a tarp
strung like a canopy over damp piles
of clothes, a campfire threading smoke between
the creekbank and a stand of river birch.

They backtracked to the road, called the police.
In woods beside our house, I started to see
blankets, bags, shoes. Was someone living there?
The creek would flood and the stuff would disappear.

Walking one day, I spotted white debris,
and what looked like thin branches whittled sharp,
spread in a tattered ring of—was it hair?

No: the strewn remains of a whitetail deer.

* * *

What did I think I'd find, or *want* to find?
What if I stumbled over some guy splayed
in leaf mold, face splotched like a mango rind?

I owned a knife, but couldn't get the blade
back in the rusted handle enough to close.
What would I do? Flail in quick jabbing heaves
to cut through his coat until I struck skin?

At home, I tugged a tangled garden hose.
I tried unkinking it. Left out too long,
the cracked vinyl had frozen to a tree.

I guess there must be people who belong,
who pull up to their faux-Victorian
in Shipshewana, crunching through dried leaves,
and think, as houselights flick on, *This is me*.

* * *

Out for a jog, I paused. I'd gone too far
along the creek the county stocked with trout.
I coughed and spit, palms planted on my knees.

Glassy with scrims of ice, a greenish foam
curdled with sulfates, reeking of chlorine.

I'd reached that time of early middle age
when I had to walk half of a five-mile run.
Now I was fifty minutes from my car
with evening coming on. Where was the sun?

I heard a honking high above the trees,
a dozen sandhills trumpeting their passage.
I squinted, kinked my neck, but couldn't see.

My wife texted, "When are you heading home?"
I turned my phone off and walked farther out.

* * *

The eight weeks she was pregnant ended in
a clotted stain on underwear she found
in a Starbucks stall. Gripping her abdomen.

She waited until after work to tell me.
"We'll try again," I said.
                    When she calmed down,
I steeped some chamomile and ordered Thai.

I cracked a window—honeysuckle musk
perfumed the evening air, peach and pear trees
expelling small damp buds that would become
yard waste our landlord mowed in summer dusk.

My wife poured out her tea and called her mom.
The door buzzed. I paid the delivery guy.

Outside, wind in the first leaves tittered like
the laugh of someone last to get a joke.

III

Exit Interview

Are you the leather bellows stoking fire
or a boy gasping after a stray kite?
Are you the edge-spar or the troposphere
tearing it free? Are you streaked like malachite
or pocked with scars? The sweaty, exigent
container of the dim confessional
or the passport photobooth, the flash's glint?
Off hours each hammer-fall misses its nail
or warning sirens whining the storm's name?
The flesh-wound fresh and throbbing or the numb
limb prickling back to life? Do you believe
the good news most have abandoned as alt-fact?
What else were you expecting to be asked?
What made you think you'd make it out alive?

Woman Waking Early in Late Fall

To meet the sun still wading through a dream
keeps her teetering between two worlds,
wearing the dream awhile like a wig of flame.
Starlings, startled from their roost, retain
the bell-shape of the tree in flits and whorls,
then scatter on a field ice-paned from rain.
The dream dissolves. There is no "thing itself."
The day increases even if starling-wheezes
remind her of the labored breathing he,
the one she dreamed, could not bear in the end—
her father's famished body on the bed,
a gnarled and desiccated specimen.

The wind shifts northward and fresh gusts efface
the tree, a sweetgum, leaving nothing left
but scab-black spikes the starlings won't refuse.
What can the sweetgum do now but accept
the murmuration tearing at its limbs
that tremble as the starlings scare and lift,
riding the same updrafts a sharp-shinned climbs?
What can she do but trace the starlings' flight
from hawk-shadow, each dive and plaintive sweep
through fog wisps thin as nebulizer mist—
these birds her father taught her how to name
before she learned to read. The starlings *zeep*.

Clutching one of their hundreds in its grip,
the hawk becomes all sharp-shinned hawks at once,
a myth of itself, stropping the cluttered sky.

Bringer of flurry-blurs and songbird slaughter,
the hawk scales altitudes on hidden rope
hung from the ozone's stratospheric rafter
in flight both circuit and circumference.
It blusters off to scarf its steaming meal,
a farther figure getting smaller faster,
appearing as a discrepancy of air,
a floater on a lens. Cloud shadows blend.
Is this the season of *before* or *after*?

On that last night her father found his speech,
an RN held a phone up to his ear—
she heard it knock against the bed's side-rail
as he hacked and gnashed his teeth repeating, "Who?"
The starlings shriek in sharp-shinned counterfeit.
A fallen feather trembles at her feet.
One letter more than *father*, further still
from *faith*, the feather gleams with oily greens
on ground too frost-shocked to admit it yet.
With autumn's insect chitters silenced now,
the sweetgum dreams the starlings back to fret
from bough to bough and crowd its vacant crown
with appetite, the sweetgum's winter fruit.

A Nonbeliever's Guide to Pascal's "Pensées"

> Inimici Dei terram lingent. *Les pécheurs lèchent la terre, c'est-à-dire aiment les plaisirs terrestres.*
> —Blaise Pascal, *Les Pensées*, fragment 666

Not that we don't lick the dust of each earthly pleasure—
even he, sitting quietly in his room alone,
must've struggled not to think of the Reblochon
tucked in the larder. It's that we can't be sure

of finding any quiet if one just sits
and listens without wanting to listen to
the traffic and HVAC huff of an afternoon
that works, like an old watercolorist,

from light to dark. Outside, a grain train drones.
Inside, the body throbs and gurgles and blurts
over a digital iron hissing at rumpled shirts,
T-Mobile jingles chirping from phones

as disposals grind lunch leavings into reeking vacancies.
Meanwhile, key fobs chirp. A mourning dove
repeats its one question (*whose? whose?*) above
livestream updates on competing vaccines.

Not to mention the Bristol/Auckland/Kokomo hum,
that low bass rumble like an idling diesel engine
so many hear. Ditto the late migration
of Canada geese honking their bugle-hymn

earbuds won't drown. No, it isn't you—
there really are more instances of "*le plaisir*"
than "*décès*" in his fragments. Which is fitting for this seer
of veins in a mite's legs, cracks in a billiard cue,

the sky's disquieting blue. Instead of quiet, why not rise
from the white noise of our lives as yet intact
and watch girders of a demo'd bridge get stacked
on semis, the snarl of cars we just as well might praise?

Self-Portrait, 2085

He doesn't look so good. Meat and marrow gone.
Buttons of his frayed shirt shedding like coins of bone
in payment for such cramped real-estate, its lease
with no option to buy, his mostly vacant sleeves
fallen open in an attitude of *what now?*
Not much from this cutaway view of nothing new.
Dust is at home anywhere. But, above, the hum
of crickets chittering summer's requiem
pauses, out of respect, for a woman who kneels
by mossy names. An automated bell knells
its know-it-all refrain. What now? Well, who can say?
Not him, effaced by the grave's false clemency,
his jaw still hinged and gaping, not as if about to speak,
but waiting, as ore waits for the pickaxe's spark.

Midlife

for my wife

What is this wanting now to know which one
will be the first, who will leave whom alone?
I scoop and spill a cup of flour again
like chalk dust on the laminate's false grain—

white as a tulle gown, white as smashed milk glass,
a gated road the town won't plow unless
it's paid, ashes on white piano keys,
smoke streaming from a cigarette's white kiss.

Outside, our neighbor forks another bale
so clean and pale it seems impossible
on bare fields luffed like sails, the hay still dry,
the flock fat with the farmer's husbandry.

Paternoster

Prague City Hall, 2003

That doorless elevator without end
rotated on a loop we waited for,
trying to step onto one of the cars
before it rose too high for us to reach it.
Stoned, we stood there watching them glide by
and still we didn't move because you said
you were scared (I was scared too but didn't say).
Then people started gathering behind us
and you told me to go—you'd take the stairs
and meet me at the top floor, "Really, go"—
then a guard insisted, *"Prosím,"* nudging us,
so we apologized and hurried on,
stumbling forward into one compartment
no larger than a water-closet stall.
Gripping each other's hand as we surged higher,
we watched each floor appear, each pair of shoes,
and reached at last the apex where the lift
rumbled and shook, went dark, flicked on its light
and shifted downward for a lower floor.

When we hopped off together on our floor
and headed for the exit and the light,
we still felt shaky, jostled by the lift,
as if the cobbles rose to meet our shoes,
cycling on some pulley climbing higher
through Old Town's vegetable and jewelry stalls,
as one feels after days at sea—the pavement

like waves repeating, dry swells bobbing on
beneath our addled staggers, both of us
joggled through avenues of vertigo
that only worsened on the rutted stairs
to Letna Park where chalkboard-smears of cirrus
blurred the blue and you asked if I could say
how long we'd stay so wobbly, then you said
the fallen almond blossoms flickering by
were white-noise pixels. I found a bench: "Let's sit."
Dodging Segways and rogue rickshaw cars,
we hummed with our ghost tremors, waiting for
the sway to wane, not wanting it to end.

The Psychoanalyst's Dream

But how shall I describe her arts
To recollect the scattered parts?
—Jonathan Swift, "A Beautiful Young Nymph Going to Bed"

By the time we arrive at the address in Broad Ripple,
the male and female guests have traded clothes.
Women, mustachioed with stick-on beards,
stab toothpicks into shriveled cocktail wieners.
Slurping appletinis, men in dresses
flinch as they cross their legs on leather settees,
itching enormous wigs heaped on their heads
like Pomeranians. A guy I know
sports a strapless gown and thigh-high boots
that strangle his legs, his face splotched red with rouge
as if he's just been slapped. He must be stoned—
he's drooling as he lectures to a ficus
about "discourses of bodily abjection."
The others look stoned, too. I recognize
the secretary of the EGO board
(our Thursday craft-beer happy-hour club)
clutching his crotch and rocking back and forth
on the hardwood, whimpering, "No more, no more."
Two women, whispering, giggle at him
as another straps a leash around his neck
and drags him from the room. Other women clap.
One of them stands on a coffee table, taps
a fork against a glass of Chardonnay
and toasts an evening of "purposive action
to destabilize the ontological

regime of presumptive phallogocentrism."
"Hear, hear!" the women shout, sipping tallboys.
Glancing at a full-length, I untuck
my heteronormative polo-shirt.
I ask Maureen if we should trade outfits,
but she's wearing skinny jeans tight as a wetsuit.
She says I wouldn't feel comfortable in heels,
reminding me about the last time she
dressed me in drag for a Halloween party—
I bitched until she finally let us leave.
I ask if we have to fight about this here.
"It's *your* night," she says. Grabbing my wrist,
she leads me to the bar where she ladles punch.
I knock it back. It tastes like molten glass.
She passes me another—I deserve it.
I'm feeling loose as I follow her downstairs
to a basement bathroom door. A woman answers.
"Giselle," Maureen says, and pecks her cheek.
I step on tiles slathered with wet hair.
Giselle fishes a razor out of the sink
and says she's "doing beards"—I should sit down.
I tell her no. Giselle, a largish woman
with a faux-hawk bleached so blonde it's luminescent,
squeezes my shoulder: "Please, sir. I insist."
She bumps her sizable belly into mine,
knocking me onto the toilet, then backs into my lap
to drop the whole brute force of her weight on me.
I can't breathe. "Now, Judith, now!" she screams.
In the tub, what seems a man in gleaming curls
swishes open the curtain and steps out
dressed in chest waders and a butcher coat

spattered with gore. Giselle says, "This is Judith."
Judith wields a large double-bladed
cigar cutter. I'm not talking about the kind
that nips the tips of Churchills—you could fit
a person's arm inside the guillotine
of this behemoth. "What's *that* for?" I say.
As Judith approaches, holding it with both hands,
she slices. The blades wheeze as they chop
like a squid's beak. Judith grins: "*Resignification*."
"Jesus," I say, "Maureen, call the police!"
Maureen says, "Sorry, muffin," and locks the bolt,
taking a butcher coat from a hook on the door.
The hook looks like a curled finger signaling
for me to come and get my punishment.
I shout, "The kids, Maureen—Christ, think of them!"
"I have," she says, "You don't want any more kids
so you don't need—Giselle, what did you call it?
His phallocentric male hegemony?"
As Judith claps my wrists in handcuffs, Maureen
complains about how often I ask for sex,
even when she's on her period.
"I'm sorry," I scream. She says she's sorry, too,
as she binds my ankles with two bungee cords
she clasps behind the toilet. I can't feel my legs.
Giselle presses her back against my chest
until my spine cracks on the toilet tank—
I swear I hear the snap of billiard balls.
"You *stink*," Giselle says, "Did you shit yourself, slave?"
Judith sets a bucket at my feet.
Inside it, shriveled nubbins of flesh writhe
like severed umbilical cords—no, cocktail wieners!

Giselle shifts her weight to unbuckle my belt—
"He *did*, he *shat* himself"—then slides my pants
over my knees, elbowing my ribs.
As Judith squats on the floor, her mouth gapes
with concentration. I see her fillings glint.
Then, a knock on the door. Maureen unlocks the bolt.
A woman in overalls apologizes
and tells us Chelsie's brought her husband, too.
"Darnell?" Giselle says, "the homophobe?"
Giselle stands up and asks me what we've learned.
"What have we *learned*?" I say, "You're fucking nuts."
Mussing my hair, she says she's disappointed,
and tells me to take my place with the other slaves.
Maureen and Judith laugh. The woman laughs.
"Enough," Maureen says, adjusting my collar:
"Let's clean you up and help you choose a dress."

On Being Mistaken for a Muslim

In college, he lived by the only mosque
in Terre Haute. Friday evenings, he'd stand
with tunicked men and women with hidden hair
who'd nod and greet him *as-salaam alaikum*
as they waited at the crosswalk for the light.
Their smiles receded when he said *hello*.

Most of the men would echo his *hello*s.
The women, never. It may have been the musk
of doused cologne he wore or the splotches of light
stubble-fuzz he thought would make him stand
out, look *cultured*, or the way he'd come
rushing to join them, still patting his wet hair,

late for one of his jobs sweeping up hair
at Supercuts or stocking shelves at Lowe's.
What kind of a person had he become
to lag and loiter there in front of the mosque,
hoping the crossing guard would let him stand
with the worshippers? They'd wave and trade polite

*Nice weather*s on the street in leaf-blotched light,
the asphalt roasting in September air
as they paused there and he tried to understand
what they said in Arabic. Soon, his *hello*s,
which he'd chirp like questions he was too shy to ask,
were converted to *wa alaikum salaam*s.

He grew bolder, offering *as-salaam alaikum*
to initiate exchanges with a slight
affectation he hoped somehow would mask
his fraud. One day, hearing the call to prayer
crackle through mounted speakers droning slow
as men crushed cigarettes beside the stand

of trees where they smoked, he hid by a newsstand
and watched men clasping hands in welcome.
One pointed at him. Another. He felt hollow.
He turned to face the street as if to slight
their fellowship, and smelled strange cooking in the air
outside the stucco security fence the mosque

installed after a car slowed one evening and
fired at the mosque's facade. When cruisers came,
spotlights found men picking glass from each other's hair.

On Emptying a Deceased Relative's Home

Some hoarders imbue the inanimate with a kind of sensibility or sentience.
—Ferris Jabr, *Scientific American*

Most objects do object to being moved:
crates of paperbacks cracking, a creaking hutch
of china the clumsy among us won't touch.
Stuck lids refuse. The hardwood, tongue-and-grooved,
groans with each step to recycling bins
distended with wire hangers and one faux-bronze bust
of Alec Douglas-Home. Mossy with dust,
pill bottles jostle against jars of safety pins.

Beyond an ample appetite for kitsch,
no theme emerges from her ten-packs of tube socks,
a snow-globe collection clinking in a liquor box,
mushroom-brim hats and cardigans that itch.
Too easy to dismiss her half-dozen heads of deer
on crooked mounts, torn Cabbage Patch dolls
with clothes she sewed herself. If estrangement dulls
familial affection, her strangeness seems to endear.

I notice we laugh less as the day progresses
from lugging trash bags of box-set Disney DVDs
through heaped-newspaper halls that make us sneeze
to hauling mattresses and folding dresses
that belonged to her daughter killed in Kandahar.
The burn pile cools. Dusk opens a pinkish wound.
Spreading blankets over boot-trampled ground,
our kids lie back and point out hole-punched stars.

Corn Poppets

for an Appalachian kitchen witch

The dead come back as braided husk and hair—
cob effigies she wraps in rags and leans
against a bedroom wall so they can hear
her griefs and grievances, their faces clean
without a mouth to make plain how she's wrong.
But when they start to flake into the floor,
the scraps she's learned to live with for so long,
those carved-stalk limbs and torsos crushed to flour,
recede, and she's offended by the loss.
Though she may tell a stone slab she forgives,
or sniff the wadded collar of a blouse,
or glimpse them in dim rooms, she knows they have
no breath or blood outside the icy stream
of these slips and dreams. Still, she slips, she dreams.

Some Problems with Autobiography

*A sensitive man, such as myself, overwhelmed by the argument
leveled against him, becomes confused and can only think clearly
again at the bottom of the stairs.*
—Diderot, *Paradoxe sur le comédien*

So far from where the stonework's slate was quarried,
the turrets crumble. The pillars won't set straight.
    Kudzu blurs what's left of the facade,
    resisting all you do, all you say.

The birds are not well-tempered. The sky, gray-green,
threatens to drown the garden you've often cursed
    for limp leeks and fertilizer burn.
    The dial's gnomon won't even cast.

Nor can you stop expanding your catalog
of friends unfriended, relatives offended,
    faces glimpsed again through gaps in mist
    as you revive quarrels with the dead.

Today, roaming the edge of the property,
you spot a child's tree fort: planks and rotting rungs
    of two-by-fours nailed along a trunk.
    You touch the scarred bark: Osage orange.

Fruit thuds to the ground, rolling the trail towards home.
At range, you can see how much the embrasures
    resemble keyholes in the tower
    you rebuilt. But certain erasures

still gape in the landscape. Pink as exposed lungs,
the attic insulation puffs from a gash
   in the roof, vibrant from last night's rain.
   Whitetails lap puddles where gutters gush.

Why not hide inside the fountain's roiled mirror?
The only angels here are granite ruins.
   Missing wings, they sulk, eroding in
   worn contortions. Their lyres plink no tunes.

Perhaps if the whitetails stayed still long enough
you might decipher some order in their dance,
   bowing out with some composure. No.
   From this purchase the view only daunts.

Instead, down valley, illegal hunters scrape
into brush a sheeting supplier owns, woods
   offering no protests to the dogs.
   What can you push against, push towards?

The foundation, this shallow shaft, was faulty
from when the contractors first poured the cement.
   They must've known the structure would warp
   under such weight. What could they have meant?

You'll find neither grace nor grouse in flushed coverts,
yet the brook carries brittle leaves the trees lost.
   What if this tale isn't yours to tell?
   What if it *is*? The stone lips stay closed.

Primer

We'd hoped it would last longer, the last year
she let us hold her sleepy in our arms,
hoist her on our shoulders to swat the air
conducting some mute fugue by Bach or Brahms.

Familiar tune, this plaint (*too soon, too soon*),
this antique ache we've struggled to oppose—
to want the morning back in afternoon
and wish for evening as the late light goes.

Though she still tells us both to tickle her,
our knees creak and our swollen ankles pop
when we tackle her, squeezing her hard to hear
the squeals that stab our eardrums: "Stop! Don't stop!"

On the drive to school, we take the backroads slow—
soon, this will all have happened long ago.

Previous Winners
of the New Criterion Poetry Prize

Nicholas Pierce, *In Transit*
Bruce Bond, *Behemoth*
Ned Balbo, *The Cylburn Touch-Me-Nots*
Nicholas Friedman, *Petty Theft*
Moira Egan, *Synæsthesium*
John Foy, *Night Vision*
Michael Spence, *Umbilical*
John Poch, *Fix Quiet*
Dick Allen, *This Shadowy Place*
George Green, *Lord Byron's Foot*
D. H. Tracy, *Janet's Cottage*
Ashley Anna McHugh, *Into These Knots*
William Virgil Davis, *Landscape and Journey*
Daniel Brown, *Taking the Occasion*
J. Allyn Rosser, *Foiled Again*
Bill Coyle, *The God of This World to His Prophet*
Geoffrey Brock, *Weighing Light*
Deborah Warren, *Zero Meridian*
Charles Tomlinson, *Skywriting and Other Poems*
Adam Kirsch, *The Thousand Wells*
Donald Petersen, *Early and Late: Selected Poems*